BECOMING LIKE JESUS

*Reflecting Christ
in Your Everyday Life*

CYNTHIA HEALD

A NavPress resource published in alliance
with Tyndale House Publishers

NavPress.com

Becoming Like Jesus: Reflecting Christ in Your Everyday Life

Copyright © 2024 by Cynthia Heald. All rights reserved.

A NavPress resource published in alliance with Tyndale House Publishers

NavPress and the NavPress logo are registered trademarks of NavPress, The Navigators, Colorado Springs, CO. *Tyndale* is a registered trademark of Tyndale House Ministries. Absence of ® in connection with marks of NavPress or other parties does not indicate an absence of registration of those marks.

The Team:
David Zimmerman, Publisher; Caitlyn Carlson, Senior Editor; Elizabeth Schroll, Copyeditor; Olivia Eldredge, Operations Manager; Eva M. Winters, Designer

Cover and interior photograph of landscape copyright © by Lukas Hartmann/Pexels.com. All rights reserved.

Interior illustration of leaves copyright © by Asya_mix/iStockphoto. All rights reserved.

Some of the anecdotal illustrations in this book are true to life and are included with the permission of the persons involved. All other illustrations are composites of real situations, and any resemblance to people living or dead is purely coincidental.

For information about special discounts for bulk purchases, please contact Tyndale House Publishers at csresponse@tyndale.com, or call 1-855-277-9400.

ISBN 978-1-64158-759-4

Printed in the United States of America

30	29	28	27	26	25	24
7	6	5	4	3	2	1

To my beloved family and friends,
who love and accept me as I seek
to become more like Jesus.

Contents

Opening Thoughts on Becoming Like Jesus

AFTER CHRISTMAS SEVERAL YEARS AGO, I went to a jewelry store to exchange a lovely bracelet I had received as a gift. Unfortunately, the bracelet had been too large for my wrist, and so the dear woman at the store very patiently helped me try on a number of bracelets. When nothing seemed to work, we began to look at earrings and necklaces instead. After about thirty minutes of searching, I finally chose a pair of earrings. At the cash register, she asked for my phone number to access my account. As she studied the screen, she suddenly asked, "Oh, are you the Cynthia Heald who writes Bible studies?"

First, I was surprised that she might know me. Then I immediately began to think, *Over the last half hour, was I nice? Was I kind? Did I exemplify someone who writes Bible studies? Was I like Jesus?*

What a humbling experience! She knew I was a Christian, and yet the whole time I was with her, I didn't even think about how I was relating to her as a Christ follower.

Although I accepted Christ as my Savior over sixty years ago and have walked with the Lord for many years, this occurrence challenged me to consider: *Am I faithful and kind in exemplifying Jesus' character to anyone I happen to encounter? Are his heart and ways so ingrained in me that I naturally reflect him to those around me, or have I become complacent, needing to be more alert and aware of God's purpose and work in my life?*

One day as I read through John's first letter to the early church, two verses seemed to be highlighted by a divine yellow marker:

Those who obey God's word truly show how completely they love him. That is how we know we are living in him. Those who say they live in God should live their lives as Jesus did.

1 JOHN 2:5-6

Living as Jesus lived—is that even possible? Jesus was sinless, performed miracles, and atoned for the sins of humanity. He was God's beloved Son! Yet here in Scripture was an incredibly specific, somewhat intimidating, and definitely challenging verse addressed to those who say they are Christ followers.

As I began to study and think about Christlikeness, one of the first places I went was the book of Ephesians, where I was reminded that it was God's will and pleasure to adopt us into his family, purchase our freedom, and forgive our sins through Jesus Christ's sacrifice on the cross (Ephesians 1:5, 7). Then in Romans 8:29, I read: "God knew his people in advance, and he chose them to become like his Son." The author of Hebrews clarified: "Therefore, it was necessary for him to be made in every respect like us, his brothers and sisters, so that he could be our merciful and faithful High Priest before God" (Hebrews 2:17).

According to these Scriptures, not only is it possible to become like Jesus, but becoming like him is God's intended purpose for his adopted children. As one biblical commentator stated:

In his character and conduct we have the clear
and complete expression of the will of the
Father. To walk as he walked is the obligation
of every one who professes to be in God.[1]

As I became increasingly convinced of my need to
be more intentional in seeking to walk as Jesus walked,
I sensed the Lord prompting me to write this devotional study. I chose to focus on God's purpose and
process of transformation, as well as the most notable
human qualities of Jesus that we have been either commanded or instructed to reflect in our lives.

In becoming like Jesus, we need to consider how
he lived and choose to imitate him. Therefore, in every
lesson of this book, we're going to ask four key questions to help us do that:

1. How did Jesus live?
2. How can we reflect him?
3. What does Scripture tell us?
4. How shall I pray?

The intent of each lesson is to encourage you as
you pursue Christlikeness, draw you in to Scripture,
and give you questions for reflection and space to write

a closing prayer. You may choose to use this book as a personal devotional and an opportunity to study and journal, or you may wish to read and discuss it as a six-week Bible study with your small group.

I found the topic of becoming like Jesus exceptionally convicting. In fact, at one point I wanted to stop writing because I realized that my family and close friends might wonder how I could ever write about what it looks like to live like Jesus! I am still very much a work in progress. This study is for me as much as it is for anyone else.

Having a personal relationship with the Lord is essential to becoming like him. As Scottish evangelist Oswald Chambers told us:

> I must know Jesus Christ as Saviour before
> His teaching has any meaning for me other
> than that of an ideal which leads to despair.
> But when I am born again of the Spirit of
> God, I know that Jesus Christ did not come
> to *teach* only: He came to *make me what*
> *He teaches I should be.*[2]

Being born again means acknowledging your need for a Savior and believing that God loved the world enough to give his only Son to die for your sins. By inviting Christ into your life to be your Savior and Lord, you become a new creation—and that is the first step toward becoming like Jesus in your daily life and interactions. You are God's adopted child, and God's purpose for you is to transform you into the likeness of his Son.

Author and pastor Richard L. Strauss urged:

> Life's highest goal for the believer is to become
> more like Christ, to allow Him to express
> more of His character and His attitudes in us.
> That is how we can fulfill our destiny and
> bring glory to God.[3]

We are invited to authentically express the Lord in our everyday lives. As we do, we will find purpose and fulfillment in experiencing God's presence and plan for us. Blessings as you bring glory to God and become all that he wants you to be—which is like Jesus.

Keep your hand in his~
Cynthia Heald

GOD'S MASTER PLAN

WE GROW IN CHRISTLIKENESS as we fix our eyes on Jesus, study how he lived, and choose to reflect him. In this lesson, we examine God's master plan, which determines our perspective on and acceptance of what happens in our everyday lives. We learn to ask ourselves: *What is his plan, and what is his purpose for me?*

How did Jesus live?

God created human beings in his own image.

GENESIS 1:27

My servant grew up in the LORD's presence
like a tender green shoot,
like a root in dry ground.
There was nothing beautiful or majestic
about his appearance,
nothing to attract us to him.

ISAIAH 53:2

Now Jesus and the ones he makes holy
have the same Father. That is why Jesus

*is not ashamed to call them his brothers
and sisters. . . .*

*Because God's children are human beings—
made of flesh and blood—the Son also became
flesh and blood.*

HEBREWS 2:11, 14

*Being in God's image means that humans
share, though imperfectly and finitely, in God's
nature, that is, in His communicable attributes
(life, personality, truth, wisdom, love, holiness,
justice), and so have the capacity for spiritual
fellowship with Him.*

ALLEN P. ROSS

Jesus, fully God and fully human, shows us what it looks like to bear God's image in human flesh. Jesus did not have anything "to attract us to him," so as God molds us into the image of his Son, we, too, are freed from worrying about our appearance or performance. We have the same Father, and we have the same Spirit within us, which means we can bear Christ's inward likeness. As we manifest his image and are increasingly shaped into Christlikeness, we carry into the world the actions and mind of Christ.

How can we reflect him?

Those whom He foreknew [of whom He was aware and loved beforehand], He also destined from the beginning [foreordaining them] to be molded into the image of His Son [and share inwardly His likeness], that He might become the firstborn among many brethren.

ROMANS 8:29, AMPC

God's ultimate purpose is that His Son might be manifested in my mortal flesh.

OSWALD CHAMBERS

In my study of becoming like Jesus, I began to search the Scriptures and read the reflections of other Christians who have explored Christlikeness. One verse in particular stood out to me. In Romans 8:29, the apostle Paul succinctly states that God's plan from the very beginning was to shape us into the image of Christ. A masterful and lofty plan! But surely this plan must be for very special, chosen people. Jesus is perfect and sinless, and to become like him seemed an impossible goal. I love the Lord and want to be who he wants me to be, but is it even possible to represent him consistently in my everyday life?

I immediately thought of one aspect of my every day: communicating with my husband. I struggle with representing the Lord consistently in this relationship, for I tend to respond too quickly and impatiently. But I know that as I desire to become like Jesus, I will begin to reflect him more and more in this area.

In the midst of my journey of becoming like Jesus, I have found encouragement from the writings of nineteenth-century pastor and author J. R. Miller:

> There are few people whom God calls to
> do great things for him, but the best thing
> most of us can do in this world is to live out

a real, simple, beautiful, strong Christian
life in our allotted place. Thus in our little
measure we shall repeat the life of the Master
himself, showing men some feeble reflection
of his sweet and loving face, and doing in our
imperfect way a few of the lovely things he
would do if he were here himself in our place.[1]

Yes! I like the words *feeble* and *imperfect* because
that is who I am. Yet I wondered about the process.
Was I doing all I could to become a moldable piece of
clay in the Lord's hands?

I was helped by this thought from pastor and author
Warren Wiersbe:

The divine "genetic structure" is already there:
God wants us to be "conformed to the image
of his Son" (Rom. 8:29). The life within will
reproduce that image if we but diligently
cooperate with God and use the means He
has lavishly given us.[2]

This is God's master plan: Empowered by the
"life within"—the Holy Spirit freely given to each of

us—we reflect Christ's life as we cooperate and yield in loving obedience to his work in conforming us.

As I gained further insight on my life as well as insight concerning God's plan, I identified four truths that can guide us as we seek to become like Jesus in our day-to-day lives:

1. Our lives find meaning and purpose as we understand that God wants to conform us to Christ.

2. When we know God's ultimate plan and his power to accomplish his purpose, we can accept and respond to the things that happen in our lives instead of spending our days resisting and reacting.

3. As we accept God's plan and yield to his Spirit within, we will experience his strength and peace when encountering trials and difficulties in this uncertain world.

4. Trusting God in all circumstances frees us and gives us confidence that God is working all things together for our good—which is to become like Jesus. As Dwight L. Moody reportedly said: "Give your life to God; he can do more with it than you can."

What does Scripture tell us?

*The success or non-success of our earthly plans
is of very little consequence in comparison with
the building up of Christ-likeness in our souls.
Do not be surprised if you fail to have your own
way at many a point. God would teach you that
true success lies in the doing of his will, not your
own, and the realizing of his plan for your life,
not your plan.*

J. R. MILLER

God's Plan

1. God intends to mold us into the image of his
   Son. How do the following Scriptures help you

understand how this plan can be implemented
in your life?

• Isaiah 64:8

_____

_____

• Luke 9:23

_____

_____

• John 14:23-26

_____

_____

• 2 Corinthians 5:17-21

_____

_____

• Ephesians 1:11-14

_____

_____

• Titus 3:4-7

_____

_____

2. As you reflect on these Scriptures and God's goal of making you like Jesus, what are some specific ways you believe that God intends to accomplish this purpose in your daily life?

_____

_____

_____

_____

Stand still awhile, and seriously consider the noble end for which thou wast created, and for which God hath placed thee in this world! Thou wast not created for time and the creature, but for God and eternity, and to employ thyself with God and eternity.

GERHARD TERSTEEGEN

Our Response

3. Recognizing that we are made for God and eternity, what do you learn from the following Scriptures about how we should respond to God's plan?

- 2 Corinthians 5:14-15

_____

_____

- Ephesians 5:1-2

_____

_____

- Colossians 3:1-4

_____

_____

- 1 Peter 3:8-9

_____

_____

- 1 John 2:5-6

_____

_____

- 1 John 3:24

_____

_____

4. We are called to be imitators of God and to live as Jesus lived. In light of these Scriptures, what changes in attitude, motivation, or action do you want to make in order to cooperate with his purpose for you?

_____

_____

_____

_____

How shall I pray?

*One day while Jesus was praying, the light
dawned on His disciples—maybe there was some
connection between the power and wisdom He
demonstrated on the one hand, and the diligence
of His prayer life on the other. So when He
finished praying, one of the disciples said to Him,
"Lord, teach us to pray" (Luke 11:1). . . . If
anyone had a right to speak on this subject, Jesus
did. He was a man of prayer. If we want to be
like Him, we too will become people of prayer.*
RICHARD L. STRAUSS

King David prayed in Psalm 138:8: "The LORD will work out his plans for my life—for your faithful love, O LORD, endures forever. Don't abandon me, for you made me." Close by writing a prayer of surrender and commitment, asking God to mold your life into the likeness of his Son.

Author's postscript

I have fond memories of playing follow-the-leader with neighborhood friends as a young girl. The game is about imitation: We all had to copy whatever our chosen leader did. If he ran, hopped, or skipped, we did the same.

Imitating Jesus as I go about my day is a challenging goal. But one commentator encourages us as we seek to pattern our lives after Jesus:

> Above all, do not be afraid of this blessed life, lived hour by hour and day by day under the guidance of thy Lord! If He seeks to bring

thee out of the world and into very close
conformity to Himself, do not shrink from it.
It is thy most blessed privilege. Rejoice in it.
Embrace it eagerly. Let everything go that
it may be thine.[3]

Because we do have God's divine genetic structure, new life through the indwelling Holy Spirit, and
our Savior's needful grace, we are equipped to reflect
Jesus' communicable attributes (aspects of his character
humans are capable of emulating) and to fulfill the
purpose for which we were created. As God's children,
it is possible to have a strong family resemblance to his
Son: This is God's plan.

My conformity to Christ is still very much an ongoing process. I must continue to guard against pride,
impatience, and complacency. I can never presume
that my past walk with God will carry me through the
present. My ability to reflect his character comes only
through a daily walk with him in which I surrender my
thoughts, actions, and plans to his will. I am humbled
at the thought of becoming like Jesus, and this divine

goal encourages me not only to accept his purpose for me but also to desire it.

In my small measure, I want to reflect the life of the Master himself. I want to live an authentic, simple, beautiful life in my allotted place. I want him to be my pattern. I don't want to miss out on the plan God has for my life. I want my responses, though imperfect and feeble, to be loving, others-centered, and gracious. I want to become like Jesus.

The best Christian is he who most reminds the people with whom he lives of the Lord Jesus Christ.
GEORGE HODGES

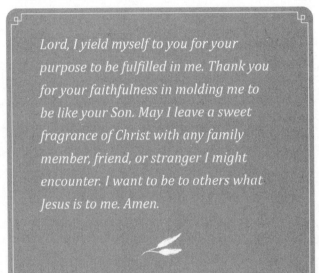

Lord, I yield myself to you for your purpose to be fulfilled in me. Thank you for your faithfulness in molding me to be like your Son. May I leave a sweet fragrance of Christ with any family member, friend, or stranger I might encounter. I want to be to others what Jesus is to me. Amen.

BEHOLDING

GOD'S MASTER PLAN is to conform us to his Son, and he accomplishes his purpose by transforming, or sanctifying, us as we become moldable in his hands. One significant element of this process is our beholding or abiding in Christ. In this lesson, we consider what beholding looks like. How, as we seek his face and his ways, do we become increasingly like Jesus?

How did Jesus live?

*The Word became human and made his home
among us. He was full of unfailing love and
faithfulness. And we have seen his glory, the glory
of the Father's one and only Son.*

JOHN 1:14

*The one thing I ask of the LORD—
    the thing I seek most—
is to live in the house of the LORD all the days
        of my life,
    delighting in the LORD's perfections
    and meditating in his Temple.*

PSALM 27:4

We have but to study the story of our Lord's life,
watching how he helped and blessed others, to
get the key to all Christian duty. His miracles we
cannot repeat, but his sympathy, his gentleness,
his thoughtfulness, his unselfishness, are patterns
for our human imitation.

J. R. MILLER

Jesus made his home among us and showed us how to
live in our world. As we endeavor to become like him,
we have his example of love, gentleness, faithfulness,
and unselfishness—all qualities that can become ours
as we study and behold him.

How can we reflect him?

1

*All of us, as with unveiled face, [because we]
continued to behold [in the Word of God] as in
a mirror the glory of the Lord, are constantly
being transfigured into His very own image in
ever increasing splendor and from one degree of
glory to another; [for this comes] from the Lord
[Who is] the Spirit.*

2 CORINTHIANS 3:18, AMPC

*The outstanding characteristic of a Christian is
this unveiled frankness before God so that the
life becomes a mirror for other lives. By being
filled with the Spirit we are transformed, and by
beholding we become mirrors.*

OSWALD CHAMBERS

I grew up in a nominally Christian home, but even as
a young girl I sensed God's presence and protection in
my life. When I was twelve years old, I accepted Christ
as my Savior and began my lifelong pursuit of becoming like Jesus.

In my early twenties I had the opportunity to grow
in Christ more deeply and intentionally. An older
woman named Mary took me under her wing and
impressed on me the all-important commandments:
to love the Lord with all my heart, soul, and mind
and to love others. She taught me to seek first the
Kingdom of God through spending time daily with
the Lord, and I learned that my primary responsibility
in the sanctification process was to behold—to gaze
at, to contemplate—the Lord, mainly through the
Scriptures. Mary talked about the authority of the
Word, showing me verses like these:

The word of God is alive and powerful. It is
sharper than the sharpest two-edged sword,
cutting between soul and spirit, between
joint and marrow. It exposes our innermost
thoughts and desires.

HEBREWS 4:12

Prophets were moved by the Holy Spirit,
and they spoke from God.

2 PETER 1:21

Years ago, I heard a unique thought about reading
the Bible. I have no idea who wrote or spoke these
words, but they are true and worth remembering: "The
Bible is the only book in the world that when you open
it, the Author shows up." The author of the Scriptures
is the Holy Spirit, and in his hands the Bible becomes
a dynamic transformational tool. That is why God's
Word isn't a mere book to be read but a way of being
transformed by beholding the glory of the Lord.

I remember Mary holding her Bible in her hand,
looking me in the eye, and saying: "Cynthia, read
through this book every year." Because I was an eager
disciple, I began my journey of beholding with a

Bible-reading plan in hand. I started reading some of the Old Testament, a psalm or proverb, and a chapter of the New Testament every day. I certainly didn't understand everything I read (and still don't), but very slowly, as I brought him an open heart, God was changing me into someone who looked more and more like Jesus.

Biblical commentator Donald Fraser exhorted us in this pursuit:

> We must form a habit of beholding that glory. We do not presume to say what amount of blessing may be gained through even a rapid or occasional glance cast on the Lord Jesus; but what the apostle intends is an habitual and daily contemplation of that "brightness of the Father's glory." No study of books, acquaintance with doctrines, or observance of rites can do for us what is done by the habit of "looking to Jesus."[1]

Beholding doesn't require education or doctrinal knowledge—it's available and accessible to each of us. All that is necessary is our desire, our choice to habitually look to Jesus.

J. R. Miller observed:

The Gospel is the mirror. There we see the
image of Christ. If we earnestly, continually,
and lovingly behold it, the effect will be the
changing of our own lives into the same
likeness. The transformation is wrought by the
divine Spirit, and our part is only to behold,
to continue beholding, the blessed beauty.[2]

I think of the four fishermen Jesus chose to be his
disciples. They were everyday men living everyday
lives, but after beholding the Lord, they were transformed and recognized "as men who had been with
Jesus" (Acts 4:13). May we be, as well.

What does Scripture tell us?

*God's method of sanctification . . . is this process
which starts from the moment of regeneration.
And it goes on and on; every experience we get
stimulates it, and we are changed from glory
to glory. We are advancing and developing. We
are to be more sanctified now than we were a
year ago and it will go on and on until finally,
in glory, we shall be perfect, without spot and
without blemish.*

MARTYN LLOYD-JONES

God's Plan

1. God's purpose is to mold and transform our
   lives so that as we behold, we become mirrors
   reflecting the image of Christ. Explore the
   following Scriptures. How does God desire to
   accomplish his plan?

   • John 17:17

   _____

   _____

   • 2 Corinthians 4:6

   _____

   _____

   • Philippians 1:6

   _____

   _____

   • Philippians 2:13

   _____

   _____

• 2 Peter 1:3-4

2. What assurance do you have concerning
   God's provision for his ongoing process of
   transformation in your life? How can this help
   you as you seek to behold the Lord?

Where there is life, there must be growth.
The new birth is not the end; it is the beginning.
God gives His children all that they need to
live godly lives, but His children must apply
themselves and be diligent to use the "means
of grace" He has provided. Spiritual growth
is not automatic. It requires cooperation with
God and the application of spiritual diligence
and discipline.

WARREN WIERSBE

Our Response

3. God is at work enabling us to grow in Christlikeness. As you study these verses, what are some ways you can respond to his process of transformation?

- Matthew 11:28-30

- Luke 9:23

- John 15:4

- Romans 12:1-2

• Ephesians 4:21-24

_____

_____

• Philippians 2:12-13

_____

_____

4. Considering what the Scriptures tell us about how
   we respond to God's process of transformation,
   what are some specific ways or areas of your life
   in which you wish to be a more diligent beholder
   and partaker in your sanctification? Write down
   what you would like to change in your daily
   choices and behaviors to accomplish this.

_____

_____

_____

_____

How shall I pray?

In Psalm 27:4, David prays: "I have asked one thing from the LORD; it is what I desire: to dwell in the house of the LORD all the days of my life, gazing on the beauty of the LORD and seeking him in his temple" (CSB). Write a prayer of commitment expressing your desire to seek the Lord and gaze on his beauty.

_____

_____

_____

_____

Author's postscript

I want to become like Jesus, but I'm wary of the process and skeptical of my own ability to be teachable. Often, God's way of conforming us to Christ involves trials—be they major or minor.

Although it was years ago, I still clearly recall one such transformative moment. My flight was delayed out of Tucson, and I realized that I would have to rush to catch my connecting flight. I was thankful I was seated toward the front of the plane; I would be able to leave quickly and, I hoped, arrive at my next gate on time.

What I hadn't counted on was having to wait for the older woman in the row in front of me. She had two carry-ons, used a cane, and was not in a hurry. After a fellow passenger and I helped her get her bag and she gathered her things, she began to *slowly* walk off the plane. I followed, but because she was pulling her suitcase and using her cane, I could not really maneuver around her. When we finally reached the terminal, I had to run to my gate. I was the last passenger to board.

As I sat in my seat, I breathed a sigh of relief and thanked the Lord that I had made it despite the frustration and difficulty of getting off the plane. But as I sat there, I sensed the Lord speaking to my heart: *Cynthia, as my child, you should have been gentle and patient with that dear lady. You could have offered to roll her bag, and you could have spoken kind and encouraging words to her. But instead you thought only of yourself.*

Contemplating the Lord's gentle chastening, I realized that I had not been a mirror reflecting the glory of the Lord at the airport. I had not laid aside my old self and sincerely presented my body as a living sacrifice. As my experience illustrates, not only does God use difficult trials to teach us to become more like Jesus, but he often uses our everyday inconveniences to humble us and point us toward Christ. I'm reminded of Chambers's observation:

> [We are] being saved in order to manifest the life of the Son of God in our mortal flesh, and it is the disagreeable things which make us exhibit whether or not we are manifesting His life.[3]

How we engage the frustrations and trials of our days is key to our transformation, and facing them with an awareness of how we are reflecting Christ requires consistent beholding. Multiple times throughout the day we experience "disagreeable" circumstances in which we have an opportunity to reflect the Lord—at work, at home, in our neighborhoods, as we shop, and, yes, as we fly! Indeed, we endure major trials, and God uses them greatly to transform us—but I find that it is the daily encounters where I am challenged the most to be patient, thoughtful, and unselfish. And when I fall short of reflecting Christ as I wish, these words from J. R. Miller encourage me:

And though but little seems to come from
our yearnings and strugglings after Christlikeness, yet God honours the yearning and
the striving; and while we sit in the shadows
of weariness, disheartened with our failures,
he carries on the work within us, and with
his own hands produces the divine beauty in
our souls.[4]

Although I continue to be disheartened by my failures, I am comforted in knowing that God continues
his transforming work; I just need to be patient. I am
reminded of the good words concerning transformation from author and lifelong missionary to India
Amy Carmichael:

So it means patience. It is not the work
of a moment. If only we allow no veils to
intervene, this transformation will go on
as steadily as the growth of a plant goes on
from hour to hour, for the Lord says it will.[5]

We may have no control over unexpected and challenging circumstances, but as we behold the Lord, we do have the assurance of the Holy Spirit's steady and continuing work in our lives to make us like Jesus—we just need to be patient and faithful in beholding him.

And so the veil which sin laid upon our sight being taken away, "we all, with open face, beholding, as in a glass, the glory of the Lord," studying His countenance, watching His looks, seeking to have His gracious and compassionate look cast upon us in the midst of our frailties and infirmities, may catch some faint reflections of its brightness, and be changed into the image whereon we gaze.

EDWARD B. PUSEY

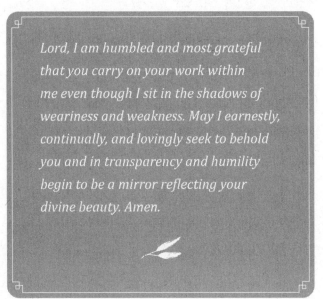

Lord, I am humbled and most grateful that you carry on your work within me even though I sit in the shadows of weariness and weakness. May I earnestly, continually, and lovingly seek to behold you and in transparency and humility begin to be a mirror reflecting your divine beauty. Amen.

HOLY OBEDIENCE

ONE OF THE STRIKING CHARACTERISTICS of Jesus was his holiness. It is also one of his qualities that we are asked to exhibit. Holiness is indeed formidable, but we must nurture it if we want to become like Jesus. In this lesson we will examine a difficult question: How is it possible to live a holy life, especially in today's world?

How did Jesus live?

This High Priest of ours understands our weaknesses, for he faced all of the same testings we do, yet he did not sin. So let us come boldly to the throne of our gracious God. There we will receive his mercy, and we will find grace to help us when we need it most.

HEBREWS 4:15-16

He never sinned,
*   nor ever deceived anyone.*

1 PETER 2:22

All who have this eager expectation will keep themselves pure, just as he is pure.

1 JOHN 3:3

It's true that He was God in human flesh and He had no sin nature, but Scripture reminds us that His temptations were real and He was "tempted in all things as we are" (Hebrews 4:15). He overcame these temptations, not because of His divine nature, but because as a man He was fully yielded to His Father's will and His Father's control.

RICHARD L. STRAUSS

Jesus, as our example, faced all the temptations we face. His victory over sin came because he was intentional in yielding himself to his Father's will. In John 8:28, he says: "I do nothing on my own but say only what the Father taught me." He was committed to living under his Father's authority and control. In his holiness, he was obedient.

How can we reflect him?

*You must live as God's obedient children. Don't
slip back into your old ways of living to satisfy your
own desires. You didn't know any better then. But
now you must be holy in everything you do, just as
God who chose you is holy. For the Scriptures say,
"You must be holy because I am holy."*

1 PETER 1:14-16

*One of the "birthmarks" of a true believer is a
hatred for sin and a desire to become more like
Jesus Christ.*

WARREN WIERSBE

My study of becoming like Jesus began with reluctance and hesitancy. I sensed that the Lord was prompting me to write, but I felt it would be too demanding. I had very good reasons, too: travel, family celebrations, company, illness, and "I'm too old!" These all seemed to be acceptable explanations. But after all my attempts to justify my uncertainty and—more to the point—my unwillingness to obey, one day I heard God's words in my heart: *I think you are out of excuses.*

As I pondered my rationalizations for not obeying God's promptings to write, I thought of how often I—and perhaps many of us—respond to the Lord's noble but exacting commands with excuses. One command that we tend to be reluctant to obey is "Be holy because I am holy." Being holy means that we are known for our godly and righteous way of life. In today's world, that is challenging, to say the least. Our lives are preoccupied with family, work, friends, and just getting through the day. Can't we occasionally call a halt to our struggle to remain moral? Shouldn't we get to indulge in a little entertainment? How can anyone possibly be holy and pure in our decadent, self-indulgent culture?

Compromise engulfs us, and we find it easier and

easier to defend our choices: *The language in the movie isn't that bad*, or *I fast-forward through any erotic scenes*, or *I skip over the steamy parts in the book*, or *This is just a friendship, and it will never go any further.*

The reality is that the world we live in abounds with temptation, for it is "under the control of the evil one" (1 John 5:19). And as James teaches in his epistle, we are naturally bent toward yielding to temptation: "Temptation comes from our own desires, which entice us and drag us away" (James 1:14). So the crucial question is: How can we, as God's "works in progress," possibly obey the command to be holy? Pastor and author Sam Storms points us to the answer:

> For the person who is born again, *the Holy Spirit has re-created you!* You are not the same person you used to be. You do not have the same desires you used to have. Your heart and mind and spirit and soul have been renewed and you are gradually being changed internally so that what you like and dislike, what you enjoy or despise, is becoming more and more like what Jesus himself experienced.[1]

We are new creations, renewed by God with a desire to follow his will and ways! We live in a sinful world, but God does not leave his children defenseless. Alongside his instruction to be holy, he provides his protection and power. Ephesians 6:10-17 describes God's provision of armor that enables us to stand firm against the devil. James 4:7 promises that when we resist Satan, he will flee from us. If we are to be holy, we must do our part: obediently putting on the armor and resisting Satan. Oswald Chambers offered this encouragement:

> God's commands are given to the life of His
> Son in us, consequently to the human nature
> in which His Son has been formed[.] His
> commands are difficult, but immediately
> [when] we obey they become divinely easy.[2]

Even with God's provision and our desire to obey, we still have to wrestle with sin in our day-to-day lives. An intriguing passage in 1 John helps us understand this tension:

> The Son of God came to destroy the works
> of the devil. Those who have been born

into God's family do not make a practice of
sinning, because God's life is in them. So
they can't keep on sinning, because they are
children of God.

1 JOHN 3:8-9

We may sin, but because we are God's children,
we will not *practice* sin. Warren Wiersbe explained:

> To "practice" sin is to sin consistently and as a
> way of life. It does not refer to committing an
> occasional sin. It is clear that no Christian is
> sinless (1 John 1:8-10), but God expects a true
> believer to sin less, not to sin habitually.[3]

When we do sin, we have the promise of 1 John 1:9:
"If we confess our sins to him, he is faithful and
just to forgive us our sins and to cleanse us from all
wickedness." Even if we feel that our former way of
life disqualifies us from being holy, accepted, or even
forgiven, God in his love gave his Son to die on the
cross to purchase our freedom and forgive our sins. By

his glorious grace, each of us has been cleansed by his blood. Second Corinthians 5:17 is true:

> This means that anyone who belongs to
> Christ has become a new person. The old life
> is gone; a new life has begun!

Even in our broken world, the presence and power of the Lord give us the weapons needed to pursue holiness. We can agree with Chambers: "It is quite true to say—'I cannot live a holy life'; but you can decide to let Jesus Christ make you holy."[4] We have a High Priest who understands our weaknesses and who gives mercy, grace, help, and forgiveness when we need them most.

What does Scripture tell us?

Remember this: God has regenerated and renewed your heart so that you would love to do what he tells you to do, he has given you his Spirit so that you would be empowered to do what he tells you to do, and he loves you beyond anything you can imagine, so never think that your suffering or his commands are anything other than expressions of his fatherly affection for you, his son or daughter.

SAM STORMS

God's Plan

1. In Leviticus 20:8, God proclaims: "I am the LORD who makes you holy." As you read the following Scriptures, what do you learn about how God produces holiness in our lives?

   • Romans 8:1-4, 12-14

   _____

   _____

   • Ephesians 6:10-17

   _____

   _____

   • Colossians 1:19-22

   _____

   _____

   • 2 Timothy 1:9

   _____

   _____

   • 2 Peter 1:3-4

   _____

   _____

• 1 John 4:4

---

2. As you reflect on these Scriptures, record the ways God is freeing you from sin and making you holy.

Our Response

We need to brace ourselves up and to realize that we are responsible for our thoughts, attitudes, and actions. We need to reckon on the fact that we died to sin's reign, that it no longer has any dominion over us, that God has united us with the risen Christ in all His power, and has given us the Holy Spirit to work in us. Only as we accept our responsibility and appropriate God's provisions will we make any progress in our pursuit of holiness.

JERRY BRIDGES

3. We are responsible for our thoughts, attitudes, and actions as we obey God in our pursuit of holiness. What encouragement or conviction do you experience from these Scriptures?

• Romans 6:12-18

• 1 Corinthians 6:18-20

• Philippians 3:12-14

• Colossians 3:5-10

• James 1:22-25

• 1 John 1:8-10

4. What do you sense you need to change in
   your life to become an obedient participant
   in becoming holy?

*Anything that leaves a taint of impurity upon the
life or starts a thought of impurity in the mind,
anything that degrades or debases the soul, is
unfit and unworthy amusement for a Christian.
Christian amusements must be such as do not
harm spiritual life; they must be means of grace.*

J. R. MILLER

How shall I pray?

In John 17:15-17, Jesus prayed for all who follow him:

> I'm not asking you to take them out of the
> world, but to keep them safe from the evil
> one. They do not belong to this world any
> more than I do. Make them holy by your
> truth; teach them your word, which is truth.

Write your own prayer asking the Lord to lead you
into his truth so you may be made holy and obedient.

Author's postscript

Without obedience, we can never pursue holiness. Missionary and author Andrew Murray remarked:

> Obedience itself is not holiness, but as the will opens itself to accept and to do the will of God, God communicates Himself and His holiness.[5]

In my pursuit of God's call to be holy, it is my responsibility to choose that which is true, honorable, and pure. I can choose righteousness, for I have been given everything needed to live a godly life. When I do obey, I experience God's blessings, which is as

Jesus taught: "Blessed are all who hear the word of God and put it into practice" (Luke 11:28).

The idea of holy obedience, though, is daunting. What will be asked of us in this pursuit? What must we sacrifice? These are reasonable questions, and if we are not careful, we will tend to view holiness as a rather dismal and joyless quest. However, nineteenth-century Scottish pastor Robert Murray M'Cheyne expressed an important perspective on what seeking holiness actually means:

> To gain entire likeness to Christ, I ought to get a high esteem of the happiness of it. I am persuaded that God's happiness is inseparably linked in with His holiness.[6]

Isn't it surprising to consider that holiness can be linked with happiness? M'Cheyne is not the only one with this insight. C. S. Lewis wrote: "How little people know who think that holiness is dull. When one meets the real thing . . . it is irresistible."[7] Scripture also confirms this truth: "Make me walk along the path of your commands, for that is where my happiness is found" (Psalm 119:35) and "The one who trusts in the LORD will be happy" (Proverbs 16:20, CSB).

So perhaps, as we travel the highway of holiness, we should do so joyfully and expectantly because it is God's love that calls us to live a holy life. He knows that the holiness he desires is the most blessed (happy),[8] satisfying, and rewarding way to live. We are created to be holy, and only our obedience will enable us to experience fulfillment, grace, and, yes, happiness—for we will be conformed to the image of his Son, who is holy, holy, holy.

In our age, as in every age, people are longing for happiness, not realizing that what they are looking for is holiness.
JERRY L. WALLS

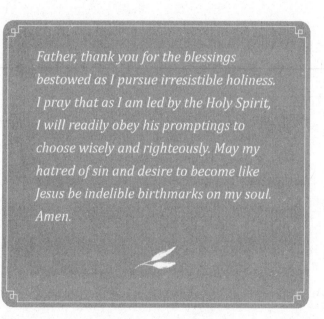

Father, thank you for the blessings bestowed as I pursue irresistible holiness. I pray that as I am led by the Holy Spirit, I will readily obey his promptings to choose wisely and righteously. May my hatred of sin and desire to become like Jesus be indelible birthmarks on my soul. Amen.

A HUMBLE SERVANT

IN THE APOSTLE PAUL'S LETTER to the Philippian church, we find these descriptive words about Jesus: "Instead, he gave up his divine privileges; he took the humble position of a slave and was born as a human being" (Philippians 2:7). Jesus entered our world as a humble servant. What should motivate us to become humble servants like Jesus?

How did Jesus live?

Then Jesus said, "Come to me, all of you who are weary and carry heavy burdens, and I will give you rest. Take my yoke upon you. Let me teach you, because I am humble and gentle at heart, and you will find rest for your souls."
MATTHEW 11:28-29

"Among you it will be different. Whoever wants to be a leader among you must be your servant, and whoever wants to be first among you must become your slave. For even the Son of Man

came not to be served but to serve others and to
give his life as a ransom for many."

MATTHEW 20:26-28

Christ came "not to be ministered unto, but to
minister," and we should be as our Lord.

J. R. MILLER

Jesus left us a vivid example of what a true servant looks like. In all his relationships and interactions, he did not seek his own fame or glory; instead, he looked for how he could serve those who came across his path. His humility and gentleness were keys to selfless service, and so it should be with us.

How can we reflect him?

Work willingly at whatever you do, as though you were working for the Lord rather than for people. Remember that the Lord will give you an inheritance as your reward, and that the Master you are serving is Christ.

COLOSSIANS 3:23-24

The mainspring of Paul's service is not love for men, but love for Jesus Christ.

OSWALD CHAMBERS

In one of his last lessons to his disciples, Jesus exemplified the marks of a true servant: humility, gentleness, and selflessness. He did this by taking off his robe, wrapping a towel around his waist, and washing the feet of the disciples. He told them:

> "Since I, your Lord and Teacher, have washed
> your feet, you ought to wash each other's feet.
> I have given you an example to follow. Do as I
> have done to you."
>
> JOHN 13:14-15

There are few things more humbling than washing someone else's feet, and by doing this, Jesus forever defined service as choosing to minister to the welfare of others with humility and for the glory of God.

A short time later in the upper room, Jesus restated his "Do as I have done to you" by instructing the disciples to love each other just as he had loved them (John 13:34). Since this command comes soon after Jesus' example of servanthood, I think that love is an integral part of serving. It should impel us to serve others, for love ennobles any service—no matter how obscure or mundane it might be. This places any service we might extend in the best light. It is the motivating force found in 1 Corinthians 13:3: "If I gave everything I have to the poor and even sacrificed my body, I could boast about it; but if I didn't love others, I would have gained nothing."

We see a follower of Jesus motivated by this kind of love earlier in the Gospel of John. Six days before the Passover, Jesus and his disciples traveled through Bethany, where Jesus' friend Lazarus lived. As they were dining in Bethany, Lazarus's sister Mary came in with a jar of expensive perfume, broke it open, and anointed the Lord with the oil (John 12:3). Jesus' disciple Judas was indignant and rebuked her for wasting the oil, which could have been sold and the money given to the poor. But Mark's Gospel records that Jesus responded with these words:

> "Leave her alone. Why criticize her for
> doing such a good thing to me? . . . She has
> done what she could and has anointed my
> body for burial ahead of time. I tell you the
> truth, wherever the Good News is preached

throughout the world, this woman's deed will
be remembered and discussed."

MARK 14:6-9

Jesus had visited the home of Lazarus, Mary, and
Martha before this encounter. He was teaching his disciples, and Mary sat at his feet and listened to his words.
As I have meditated on Mary's choices—to listen to his
teaching and then to anoint him—I've come to believe
she grasped the truth that Jesus was going to die. I think
she pondered in her heart, *How can I show Jesus how much
I love him? I know—I'll anoint his body for burial.* And
Jesus commended her for this heartfelt, extravagant gift
expressing her immense love and reverence for the Lord.

Mary's actions give us a priceless lesson to consider
as we seek to be humble servants. Mary humbled her-
self and thought only of Jesus; she was not concerned
about what people might say or think. Abiding at the
feet of Jesus was what prompted her to anoint the Lord
and to give what she could to bless him. Perhaps true
service is not showing people how much we love Jesus,
but showing Jesus how much we love him.

As Andrew Murray wrote:

Abiding in Jesus, let us live like Him, washing
one another's feet and even giving our lives for
others. Let us find our highest joy in blessing
others and yield ourselves regularly to the
Holy Spirit so that we are constantly learning
the divine love. The commonplace parts
of our lives will be infused with a heavenly
beauty as we do these things.[1]

What does Scripture tell us?

It is the servitude of my God-occupied heart.
He has come Himself and made His abode in
me, through His Holy Spirit given to me. From
within He rules me far more than from without.
And so, rejoicingly and inevitably and eternally,
I yield myself to Him.

ALEXANDER SMELLIE

God's Plan

1. God's plan is for us to become like Jesus—
   the righteous servant who gave up his divine
   privileges and took the humble position of a slave.
   Explore the following Scriptures. What are the
   desired qualities of a gentle and lowly servant?

   • Matthew 25:22-23

   _____

   _____

   • Mark 10:42-45

   _____

   _____

   • John 12:26

   _____

   _____

   • John 13:12-15

   _____

   _____

- 1 Corinthians 10:23-24

2. As you consider Jesus' invitation, teaching,
   and example, what specific steps can you take
   to consistently grow in becoming a humble
   and gentle servant?

*Christ became what we are that he might make
us what he is.*

SAINT ATHANASIUS OF ALEXANDRIA

Our Response

3. Study these verses in light of our ongoing
   transformation. What specific ways do we need to
   respond in order to become servants?

- 1 Corinthians 15:58

- Galatians 5:13-14

- Ephesians 4:2

- Philippians 2:3-4

- Philippians 2:14-18

- Colossians 3:22-24

• James 3:13, 17-18

_____

_____

4. As you reflect on the servitude of your God-
   occupied heart, choose one or two Scriptures to
   record here. How can you begin applying these
   verses to your everyday activities?

_____

_____

_____

_____

5. What encourages you to work willingly even at
   ordinary, simple things to show that, above all,
   you love Jesus?

_____

_____

_____

_____

How shall I pray?

In Romans 12:10-11, Paul writes to the church:

> Love each other with genuine affection, and
> take delight in honoring each other. Never
> be lazy, but work hard and serve the Lord
> enthusiastically.

Using these verses, write your prayer that these
qualities may become more and more evident in your
life as you serve.

_____

_____

_____

_____

Author's postscript

We could study a multitude of perspectives on serving and being a servant, but instead I wanted to present the essential foundation of serving: a humble, gentle, self-sacrificing love. This "spirit of service" frees us to serve spontaneously and purposefully in whatever role or circumstance we find ourselves in. To have this spirit of service, though, we must be like Mary and sit at the feet of Jesus: We must behold him. We can become like Jesus because he invites us to learn from him.

In my serving, I am not always as free and spontaneous as I would like. I tend to be fairly willing and patient if I have chosen when and where I wish to serve, but so often if I am interrupted or intruded upon by unexpected circumstances that demand my service, I find myself becoming frustrated and impatient.

When I encounter these unplanned opportunities to serve (usually within my family), I pray a rather feeble but truthful prayer: "Lord, if I didn't love you, I wouldn't be doing this." I have found this honest prayer helps my attitude and my actions as I serve— because love for the Lord should be the mainspring of my service. As I pray and focus on expressing my love for the Lord, I am drawn to humble myself and to look after the interests of others.

I've always liked how the parable of the Good Samaritan offers an example of how to serve. Not only did the Samaritan stop to help the wounded man on the road, but he also took him to an inn and provided for his continued care through the innkeeper. I have learned two important lessons from this parable:

1. We don't need to be so pressed for time that we can't stop to serve the needy who happen to cross our path.

2. It is good to enlist other people to help, especially if we have a prior commitment with someone else at that time. Serving is priceless and a blessing, but it should not monopolize our time to the extent that we neglect our existing duties. I think of the apostles, who realized that their responsibilities were to pray and teach the Word to the early church and consequently asked for seven men to be appointed to serve the widows in the daily food distribution (Acts 6:1-4).

Humble servants are willing to serve wherever they sense a need. I once heard about a dear woman who wanted to share Christ with and serve the women in a nearby prison. For several weeks, she met and visited with a few of the inmates. Eventually she began a Bible study with a small group there. During her time visiting the prison, she kept noticing one inmate who appeared curious but always kept her distance. After everyone left the first Bible study, the watchful but reticent observer approached her and quietly said, "I want what you have." And, of course, what she had was Jesus.

No one gives himself freely and willingly to God's service unless, having tasted his fatherly love, he is drawn to love and worship him in return.

JOHN CALVIN

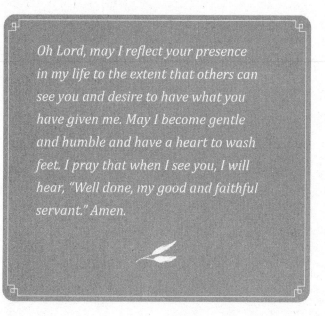

Oh Lord, may I reflect your presence in my life to the extent that others can see you and desire to have what you have given me. May I become gentle and humble and have a heart to wash feet. I pray that when I see you, I will hear, "Well done, my good and faithful servant." Amen.

UNCONDITIONAL LOVE

GIVING UNCONDITIONAL LOVE was Jesus' way of life. In this lesson, we behold Christ's sacrificial love and his forgiveness of our sin. What are we called to do in following Jesus in the daily practice of unconditional love?

How did Jesus live?

"Now I am giving you a new commandment: Love each other. Just as I have loved you, you should love each other. Your love for one another will prove to the world that you are my disciples."

JOHN 13:34-35

Imitate God, therefore, in everything you do,
because you are his dear children. Live a life
filled with love, following the example of Christ.
He loved us and offered himself as a sacrifice for
us, a pleasing aroma to God.

EPHESIANS 5:1-2

Christ alone is the perfect Example; he loved
his people with a constant, patient, and
forbearing love; with a love active, practical,
and self-sacrificing. As he loved us, so he expects
us to love one another.

J. R. THOMSON

Because Jesus left us a faithful example of loving in everyday life, we are asked to imitate him. We are to be patient, forbearing, and sacrificial as we love. We can do this because of the indwelling Holy Spirit, whose first fruit in our lives is love.

How can we reflect him?

1

*This is real love—not that we loved God, but
that he loved us and sent his Son as a sacrifice to
take away our sins. Dear friends, since God loved
us that much, we surely ought to love each other.*

1 JOHN 4:10-11

*We are to imitate God's love in Christ. The love
that gives, that counts no cost too great, and, in
sacrificing itself for others, offers all to God, and
does all for His sake. Such was the love of Jesus.*

F. B. MEYER

I tend to be self-conscious when being introduced. One time, a conference director commented to the group, "Cynthia loves women," and I gasped inwardly. Yes, true, I do love some women, but I thought it an overstatement to say I love women in general. I realized that ingrained in me were some conditions that had to be met before I extended love: I liked my space, I didn't like interruptions, I didn't enjoy small talk, and it was hard for me to "forbear." I wanted to be loving, but as I examined my motives, I discovered I usually loved when I thought the other person was worthy and deserved it. Yet here I was introduced as a woman who loved others. Knowing that Jesus commanded us to love as he loved, I realized the question I needed to answer was: How did he love?

When I compared a few of my conditions for loving others with the love Jesus portrayed, I found that he had no space—no place to lay his head. Jesus was continually interrupted (as someone once said, he had a ministry of interruptions): by a woman with an issue of blood, by the disciples during a time of prayer, by a paralytic while teaching. When he met people, he engaged with each one truthfully, personally, and patiently—we see his forbearance with the woman at the well and the pharisee Nicodemus. As I looked at his life, I found that he loved *un*conditionally. He took time with everyone; it didn't matter whether they were "worthy" or not.

Challenged by the way Jesus loved, I began my mission to love by praying: "Okay, Lord, I'm going to start loving others because you have asked me to." My intent was good, but I was not very successful. There seemed to be no joy when I attempted to love with that attitude. Then one day, I sensed the Lord speaking to my heart:

Cynthia, if you want to love as I love, you must remember first and foremost how much you are loved. I purchased you; you were bought with a price. My death on the cross redeemed you; your sins are forgiven, and you are now united with me. I have loved you even as the Father has loved me. Remain in my love. When you obey, you have my love to give. When you bestow the gift of my love upon others, you are fulfilling the purpose for which you were created, and you are blessed. You will experience joy most often when you love unconditionally and selflessly with no thought of receiving anything in return—for this is the way I love you.

This love Jesus exemplified is *agapē* love. Greek New Testament scholar Kenneth Wuest described *agapē* love in this way:

> [*Agapē* love is] the love which the Holy Spirit sheds abroad in the heart of the yielded believer.[1]

And in his Greek word study on the word, Bible study teacher Bruce Hurt explains:

> [*Agapē*] love does not derive its motivation from the desirability of the object of one's affection but gives with no expectation of return (unconditional) so that if given and not returned then you don't stop giving it.[2]

Unquestionably, the supreme illustration of *agapē* love is Jesus' sacrifice on the cross. In Ephesians 1:7, we read: "He is so rich in kindness and grace that he purchased our freedom with the blood of his Son and forgave our sins." To let us be righteous before him and receive forgiveness for our sins, God so loved the world that he gave his only Son to redeem us. Forgiveness is inextricably bound with love.

We read in Romans that "God showed his great love [*agapē*] for us by sending Christ to die for us while we were still sinners" (Romans 5:8). And the apostle John wrote: "Since God loved us that much, we surely ought to love each other" (1 John 4:11). Because of the forgiveness we have received, we are to imitate Christ, forgiving others with no expectation of a response. Colossians 3:13-14 teaches:

> Make allowance for each other's faults, and forgive anyone who offends you. Remember, the Lord forgave you, so you must forgive others. Above all, clothe yourselves with love [*agapē*], which binds us all together in perfect harmony.

Jesus taught the primacy of forgiveness in Mark 11:25: "When you are praying, first forgive anyone you are holding a grudge against, so that your Father in heaven will forgive your sins, too." A bitter, revengeful spirit distances us from God and becomes a barrier in our relationship with him. Again, I think that God asks us to forgive because it is the best thing for us. Forgiveness frees the forgiver and is not dependent on the responses of those we forgive. As our Father, God takes full responsibility for our well-being:

> Dear friends, never take revenge. Leave
> that to the righteous anger of God. For the
> Scriptures say,
>
> "I will take revenge;
>   I will pay them back,"
>   says the LORD.

ROMANS 12:19

The gift of *agapē* love and forgiveness "has been poured out in our hearts" (Romans 5:5, CSB)—and what we have received we are to give to others, unconditionally, as Jesus did.

> *Jesus is giving us a completely different way to live, and it's one that sets us free from anger, free from ever-present guilt, free to really love people, free from constant anxiety, and free to get a good night's sleep.*

BRANT HANSEN

What does Scripture tell us?

Loving means doing what is right from God's point of view. We can only know His viewpoint when we live in His presence and fill our minds with His Word.

RICHARD L. STRAUSS

God's Plan

1. Jesus gave a new commandment: to love others as he loves us. As you explore these Scriptures, what further instructions or promises about loving others do you observe?

- Matthew 22:37-40

- Romans 5:8-11

- Romans 8:35-39

- Ephesians 2:4-7

- Ephesians 3:14-19

- 1 John 4:15-21

---

2. The apostle John wrote: "We love each other because he loved us first" (1 John 4:19). Write a summary of how God has expressed his love for you personally.

> *"Who is thy neighbor?" It is the sufferer, wherever, whoever, whatsoever he be. Wherever thou hearest the cry of distress, wherever thou seest any one brought across thy path by the chances and changes of life (that is, by the Providence of God), whom it is in thy power to help,—he, stranger or enemy though he be, —he is thy neighbor.*
>
> A. P. STANLEY

Our Response

3. God commands us to love our neighbor. Study the following verses. What actions should we take to receive *agapē* love or express it to others?

- Matthew 6:9-15

_____

_____

- Luke 6:27-36

_____

_____

- John 14:21

_____

_____

- John 15:9-10

_____

_____

- 1 Corinthians 13:1-7

_____

_____

- Galatians 5:22-23

_____

_____

• 1 Peter 4:8-9

_____

_____

4. In what ways do these Scriptures challenge you,
   whether in your actions or attitudes, to love
   like Jesus?

_____

_____

_____

5. From his glorious, unlimited resources and
   through his Spirit, God empowers us with inner
   strength. In what ways can you begin to purposely
   apply *agapē* love to your everyday life? Is there
   someone you need to forgive, someone you can
   serve, someone you can comfort, or someone you
   can befriend?

_____

_____

_____

How shall I pray?

To the Ephesian church Paul writes a beautiful prayer, asking that their roots may go down deep into God's love. Carefully read Ephesians 3:16-19 and use these verses to create a prayer for yourself.

Author's postscript

Oh, the incredible gift of knowing that we are loved. God is love (1 John 4:8). God so loved the world that he gave (John 3:16). His love is undeserved, everlasting, steadfast, and faithful, and he lavishes it on us. We no longer have to look for love in all the wrong places. We no longer need to feel unworthy, guilty, ashamed. Nothing can separate us from God's love (Romans 8:38). We love because he first loved us (1 John 4:19). We are complete in Christ and now have the blessing of giving unconditional love to others. Only as we look to God as our source of love and love him with all our hearts, minds, and souls can we love others well. As pastor and counselor Maurice E. Wagner wrote:

> Obeying the first great commandment redeems us from the bondage of self-verification. . . . Instead of loving others because we need to be loved by them, we find ourselves loving others because we are loved by God, and most of all, we feel loving. . . . So we no longer maneuver to prove ourselves to others . . . to gain status . . . or to avoid criticism.[3]

Our freedom has been purchased with the sacrificial love of Christ. When we obey the Lord's commands, we remain in his love and are empowered to bestow his love on others. By remaining in Christ's love, we are freed from condemnation and the irritation of interruptions, freed from having to manipulate others to love us, freed from self-absorption, freed from bitterness. Now we are free to love unconditionally like Jesus, free to give this precious gift of love to all we meet on our journey, free to experience joy, and free to bring God glory.

*When by simple faith I accept Christ's shed blood
as full payment for my sins, I am brought into a
relationship with an infinite Being of love and
purpose who fully satisfies my deepest needs for
security and significance. Therefore I am freed
from self-centered preoccupation with my own
needs; they are met. It is now possible for me
to give to others out of my fullness rather than
needing to receive from others because of my
emptiness. For the first time, I have the option
of living selflessly.*

LAWRENCE J. CRABB, JR.

Dear Father, how gracious you are to love me sacrificially, unconditionally, and eternally. Thank you for freeing me to love as you have loved me. I ask that as I love others, they may see Jesus. Amen.

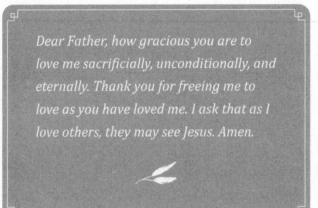

TRUSTING GOD'S PLAN

SCRIPTURE RECORDS THAT JESUS humbled himself in obedience to God (Philippians 2:8). We have Christ's example to follow in trusting our Father's will. Our final lesson will explore this question: How do we become like Jesus, who trusted God in and through every part of his life, even in trials and sufferings?

How did Jesus live?

"I have come down from heaven to do the will of God who sent me, not to do my own will."

JOHN 6:38

Since he himself has gone through suffering and testing, he is able to help us when we are being tested.

HEBREWS 2:18

The reason that Jesus is in such close solidarity with us is that the difficult path we are on is not unique to us. He has journeyed on it himself.

DANE ORTLUND

Jesus was committed to doing God's will, and as the Son of Man he journeyed on the difficult path of suffering and testing. We can live as he did, for he knows what it is like to trust our Father within our fragmented world.

How can we reflect him?

Trust in the LORD with all your heart;
   do not depend on your own understanding.
Seek his will in all you do,
   and he will show you which path to take.

PROVERBS 3:5-6

We know that God causes everything to work
together for the good of those who love God and
are called according to his purpose for them.

ROMANS 8:28

To believe actively that our Heavenly Father constantly spreads around us providential circumstances that work for our present good and our everlasting well-being brings to the soul a veritable benediction.

A. W. TOZER

At one of the first conferences where I spoke, attendees were asked to evaluate the speaker afterward. While I had some public-speaking experience, I had never been evaluated before, as far as I knew. But this time I was given the evaluations to read. As I scanned several pages, my heart seemed to stop when I read:

- "I did not like the speaker."
- "This speaker was too serious."
- "I liked the speaker you had last year."

To a confirmed people pleaser, these were devastating and painful words. Immediately I told the Lord, "I am never speaking in front of a crowd again."

God graciously gave me time to process these honest but wounding words. Eventually, I sensed his thoughts, and we had this conversation:

Cynthia, if I want you to speak and no one likes you, will you speak anyway?

"Oh, no, Father, I don't want to speak if no one likes me."

But if it is my will for you to speak my truth, will you do it just for me?

"I don't know—can I think about it?"

As I began reflecting on that upsetting and humiliating experience, the Holy Spirit impressed upon me that his sanctification process required my unshakable trust during such unforeseen circumstances. Oswald Chambers addressed my quandary in this way:

Am I willing to reduce myself simply to "me," determinedly to strip myself of all my friends think of me, of all I think of myself, and to hand that simple naked self over to God? Immediately I am, He will sanctify me wholly, and my life will be free from earnestness in connection with every thing but God.[1]

I realized that God was using this experience to sanctify me and free me from seeking approval from people, inviting me instead to seek approval from him.

God wanted me to trust that whatever trial came into my life would be for my present good and my everlasting well-being.

The author of Hebrews wrote of the blessing of God's transforming process:

> God's discipline is always good for us, so that
> we might share in his holiness. No discipline
> is enjoyable while it is happening—it's painful!
> But afterward there will be a peaceful harvest
> of right living for those who are trained in
> this way.
> HEBREWS 12:10-11

And Warren Wiersbe reminded us that as we are being transformed, we may often encounter adversity:

> God's love for His own is not a pampering
> love; it is a perfecting love. The fact that He
> loves us and we love Him is no guarantee
> that we will be sheltered from the problems
> and pains of life. After all, the Father loves
> His Son: and yet the Father permitted His
> beloved Son to drink the cup of sorrow and
> experience the shame and pain of the cross.

We must never think that love and suffering
are incompatible. Certainly they unite in
Jesus Christ.[2]

Yes, love and suffering unite in Jesus, and because
of this we can become like him, for he traveled the
same difficult roads we travel. We can reflect the confi-
dent abandon and trust that Jesus had when he entered
our world not to do his will but to do the will of his
Father. As Peter reminds us: "God called you to do
good, even if it means suffering, just as Christ suffered
for you. He is your example, and you must follow in
his steps" (1 Peter 2:21).

God's master plan is to make us like Jesus—to teach
us to follow in his steps—and we are promised that
God will work everything together for the good of
those who love him and are called according to his purpose (Romans 8:28). We must believe, we must trust,
we must remember that God works even our suffering
for our good—and the good and the purpose he is after
is conformity to the likeness of his Son.

What does Scripture tell us?

To those, whose hope is in heaven, everything becomes a means of discipline, an instrument of strengthening their cheerful acceptance of their Father's will. Their irksome tasks, privations, sickness, heaviness of heart, unkindness of others, and all the sorrows which their Father allots them in this world, are so many means of conforming them to their Saviour's image.

EDWARD B. PUSEY

God's Plan

1. The psalmist proclaimed: "How precious are your thoughts about me, O God. They cannot be numbered!" (Psalm 139:17). What do the following verses reveal about God's care and love for you?

• Psalm 25:8-10

_____

_____

• Psalm 84:11-12

_____

_____

• Isaiah 26:3

_____

_____

• Ephesians 2:10

_____

_____

• Hebrews 13:5-6

_____

_____

• Hebrews 13:20-21

_____

_____

2. God is committed to using everything in your life as a means of conforming you to his Son. How do these verses encourage you to trust him?

_____

_____

_____

Faith in God will not get for you everything you may want, but it will get for you what God wants you to have.
VANCE HAVNER

Our Response

3. Ephesians 5:17 tells us: "Don't act thoughtlessly, but understand what the Lord wants you to do." According to these verses, what is required to act thoughtfully in order to do God's will?

• Psalm 37:5

• Psalm 143:10

• Proverbs 3:5-6

• Romans 12:2

• 2 Corinthians 4:16-18

_____

_____

• Philippians 1:29

_____

_____

• Hebrews 10:35-36

_____

_____

4. What trials have you experienced (or are you presently enduring)? How have these Scriptures addressed your experiences? How have they encouraged you?

_____

_____

_____

_____

In my daily life I am to ask "How would Christ *have acted in my circumstances? How would He have me act? How would* Christ *fulfill my duties, do my work, fill my place, meet my difficulties, turn to account all my capacities and opportunities?" . . . There is to be a manifestation of the Divine Nature in* me.

A. C. A. HALL

5. What do you sense the Lord prompting you to do as you seek to increase your trust in his master plan for your life, even if it involves suffering?

_____

_____

_____

_____

How shall I pray?

These prayerful words are found in Psalm 143:8: "Let me hear of your unfailing love each morning, for I am trusting you. Show me where to walk, for I give myself to you." Following the example of this prayer, write your own prayer for wholehearted trust: that you may in faith embrace the providential circumstances that come into your life and grow in manifesting the divine nature in you.

_____

_____

_____

_____

_____

Author's postscript

The night before his crucifixion, Jesus spoke these parting words to his disciples: "I have told you all this so that you may have peace in me. Here on earth you will have many trials and sorrows. But take heart, because I have overcome the world" (John 16:33). We need to remember these trustworthy words, for trials are to be expected here on earth—for believers and nonbelievers alike. No one is exempt.

But we who trust the Lord can take heart because Jesus has overcome the world. As we encounter sorrow and suffering, we have his peace and the assurance of God's presence: "I will never fail you. I will never abandon you" (Hebrews 13:5); "When you go through deep waters, I will be with you. When you go through rivers of difficulty, you will not drown" (Isaiah 43:2). Even Jesus shared: "The one who sent me is with me—he has not deserted me. For I always do what pleases him" (John 8:29). When we face hard times, God strengthens us with the reminder that we are never alone. He is always with us—loving us, comforting us, guiding us, and using all we contend with for his eternal purpose and our good.

Joseph is an excellent example of this truth. He was betrayed by his brothers and sold into slavery, yet Scripture states: "The LORD was with Joseph, so he succeeded in everything he did" and "The LORD was with Joseph in the prison and showed him his faithful love" (Genesis 39:2, 21). Because of God's presence in his life and his trust in God's plan, Joseph could say to his brothers when meeting them years later: "You intended to harm me, but God intended it all for good" (Genesis 50:20). Joseph's life exemplifies the certainty that God overrides adversity, is always with us, and works all things for good.

Although I have never been imprisoned, I have undergone multiple trials—some much harder to endure than poor evaluations. These trials have taught me that God uses suffering for his purposes. I know the truth of J. R. Miller's observation:

> Every experience of suffering ought in some way to lift us nearer to God, to make us more gentle and loving, and to leave the image of Christ shining a little clearer in our lives.[3]

As I travel the unpaved roads on my journey, I don't always understand God's ways. But my hope is that as he redeems my suffering, the image of Christ will shine a little clearer in my life: for I know that "a successful life in the end is one which has done that for which God created it."[4] And God created us to become like Jesus and to reflect him in our everyday lives.

Wondering if there is any reason or purpose for you to take up space on this care-worn planet? The mystery is unraveled in Him as He scripts your life to be lived for His glory and to reflect the radiance of His character.
JOSEPH M. STOWELL

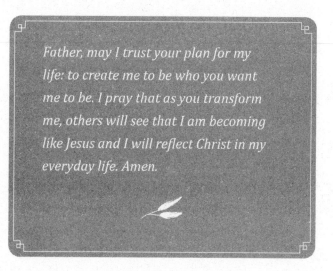

Father, may I trust your plan for my life: to create me to be who you want me to be. I pray that as you transform me, others will see that I am becoming like Jesus and I will reflect Christ in my everyday life. Amen.

Closing Thoughts
on Becoming Like Jesus

*A Christian visiting in the Soviet Union during
a period of oppression had the opportunity to talk
to a group of persecuted believers there. When he
asked them what prayer requests he could share
with his friends in the States on their behalf, they
replied, "Pray that we would be more like Jesus."*
RICHARD L. STRAUSS

IF SOMEONE ASKS YOU HOW THEY CAN PRAY for
you, how do you answer? My hope is that my instinctive answer increasingly becomes "That I would
become more like Jesus," for this is God's purpose. I
pray that it will be your answer as well. His plan to
conform us to Christ gives us the security we desire as
we navigate this world, for he is always with us. As we

walk his path, we can be assured that all that comes into our lives is for our highest good.

The apostle Paul affirmed this certainty: "I am sure of this, that he who started a good work in you will carry it on to completion until the day of Christ Jesus" (Philippians 1:6, csb). What an incredible thought to know that God will complete his plan of conforming us to Christ! We must remember, though, that his master plan is contingent on our making two crucial choices: to abandon our lives to him, and to trust him wholeheartedly. Major W. Ian Thomas emphasized the importance of our trust and surrender:

> Though He is God Himself, the Holy Spirit
> has chosen always to govern your behavior
> and exercise supreme control in every part of
> your being *only by your own free choice and
> glad consent.*[1]

The choice is ours. May we gladly consent to become like Jesus and reflect him in our everyday lives, and may we become his children who continually pray:

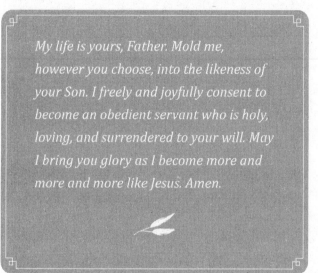

My life is yours, Father. Mold me, however you choose, into the likeness of your Son. I freely and joyfully consent to become an obedient servant who is holy, loving, and surrendered to your will. May I bring you glory as I become more and more and more like Jesus. Amen.

Those who obey God's word truly show how completely they love him. That is how we know we are living in him. Those who say they live in God should live their lives as Jesus did.

1 JOHN 2:5-6

A Conversation
with Cynthia Heald

by Joyce Koo Dalrymple, author of
Women of the New Testament and *Jesus' Passion Week*
(LifeChange Bible Studies)

JOYCE

Cynthia, I was introduced to your Bible studies in probably the 1990s. And I think yours may have been the first women's Bible studies I'd ever done. I still remember them because your studies really lit a desire in me to study the Word. Here I am now all these years later, writing Bible studies. And you're still writing Bible studies!

CYNTHIA

Over and over, I keep telling the Lord, "I'm too old to write." He hasn't gotten the message. That's why in this book, I originally entitled the last part "The Final Postscript." I said, "Lord, I hope you are taking note of this."

JOYCE

You've been writing Bible studies since 1986, almost forty years. How did God originally place that burden on your heart to start writing these Bible studies and leading people into a deeper dive of Scripture?

CYNTHIA

When I turned forty, I realized that my life was probably half over. It had gone so quickly! I said, "Oh, Lord—if my life is half over, then I just want you to know I don't want to miss out on anything you have for me. These first forty years went so fast. I want to be in the center of your will for the rest of my life, as much as I can."

As I read through Scripture that year, I got to Ruth, which I had read many times, and I read where Ruth was known as a "woman of excellence" (Ruth 3:11, NASB) or a "woman of noble character" (Ruth 3:11, CSB). And I asked, "Lord, when did you put that verse in there? I never saw it before!" And then I asked, "How could Ruth be known as a woman of excellence?" She was a widow. She was living with an unhappy mother-in-law, she was in a foreign country, and she was on the lowest social scale of that country, which was being a foreign widow. She should have been known as "poor widow Ruth." Yet everyone who knew her said, "Oh, yes, Ruth—she's a woman of excellence."

I told the Lord, "I don't know what a woman of excellence is, but I want to find out, and I want to be in the process of becoming a woman of excellence for the rest of my life." When people have asked, "Oh, what'd you major in during college?" and I say, "In English," they say, "Oh, no wonder you write." I say, "No, I majored in English because I like to read. It's not because I like to write." So the study was all for me.

I had four teenagers. This was before computers. I got a yellow pad out and wrote for two years. I wasn't in a hurry. I wrote a course called *Becoming Women of Excellence* and taught it to the women at our church, and that was it.

NavPress heard I had done this and asked for my notes. I sent them in, and next thing I knew, they said, "Do you want this to be a book or a Bible study?" I told NavPress, "Well, I guess it needs to be a Bible study because the Bible is the only thing that changes our lives, not anything I have to say." They said, "Okay. Write a Bible study." It took another two years, I think. Again, I had four teenagers. I wasn't in a hurry.

JOYCE

Once you got *Becoming a Woman of Excellence* out there, did you have a desire to write more?

CYNTHIA

After *Becoming a Woman of Excellence* came out, I didn't think about it anymore. But my prayer was, "Lord, I'd like to go deeper with you." And in response, I sensed God prompting me with this thought: "Well then, if you want to go deeper, why don't you do a Bible study in the Psalms?"

And I said, "There are 150 psalms, and I don't know anything about these." This woman gave me Charles Spurgeon's *The Treasury of David* out of the blue. It was like God said, "Yes, I want you to study this."

Eventually, some of the Bible studies were being used in churches, and people started asking me to come speak. One afternoon, Jack, my husband, came and gave me his dry-cleaning ticket and said, "Cynthia, you can pick up my clothes after four o'clock tomorrow afternoon."

I didn't say anything at first. I took the ticket. And then I said, "Okay." But in my heart, I said, *You know what? You took them, you pick them up. I'm starting to do a little traveling and speaking, and you're a healthy, mature adult. You can go get your own clothes.*

I didn't say that, praise God. But God heard, and it was so clear. He said, "Cynthia, you have got to write a study on loving your husband."

Later, I felt the Lord prompting me to write a study on prayer. And I told God, "God, I know absolutely nothing about prayer. I am not a prayer warrior. I can't write a study on prayer." And he said, "I know—that's exactly why you need to do it."

For all my writing, I feel like this is what God said: "The only way Cynthia's going to begin to be conformed to the image of Christ is to have her write Bible studies. This is the only way she's going to learn anything."

So all the Bible studies are for me. This last one, I said, "Lord, you have a great sense of humor. I'm eighty-four years old, and you're having me write about becoming like Jesus, which I need. Thank you that you think I still have a few years left to become more like Jesus."

I've never thought, *What do women need and what can I write?* I've always written out of obedience to God for what he wants to teach me.

JOYCE

I love that, Cynthia. It's so like God to love us so much that he would give you tailored assignments—and that he would then use those assignments to feed and bless so many other people. He's blessing you first and feeding you first, and then using those loaves and fish to multiply that out.

What is a favorite story you have received from someone who read your books or did your study?

CYNTHIA

It's been such a blessing to meet women—like you, Joyce!—who say, "Yours was the very first Bible study I ever did, and it really has laid a foundation in my life." That means so much. When I wrote *Becoming a Woman of Excellence*, nobody knew that it might be used in high school or college. Nobody but God knew.

I have a friend who was doing a ministry in the women's prison in Houston. Years ago she took ten inmates through my study *Becoming a Woman of Freedom*. Each of the inmates wrote me a note, and I still have them. That has been so precious to me—that these women could study the Word and share with and encourage one another, and that I could be a tiny part of that. I did go into prison one evening and share Christ, and that was very special. I still pray for those dear ladies.

I had another friend who knew someone who was getting a divorce, and my friend said, "Before you go through with this divorce, why don't you and I do this study *Loving Your Husband*?" And the woman said, "Okay." This woman even wrote me after doing the study. She did not get a divorce, and she's still married.

I stand amazed at God because of things like that. Because again, it is his Word. It's Scripture that changes lives, not anything I think. So I treasure those stories— opportunities I would never have thought of or thought that God could use, but that's what he does, Joyce, with our studies. That's what's so neat.

JOYCE

What encouragement do you have for someone who has this kind of calling—writing or teaching people how to study Scripture? What challenge or caution do you have?

CYNTHIA

Well, again, this answer applies to me and not to anybody else, but it's the best answer I have. I was doing a question-and-answer time at a conference, and this one lady stood up and asked, "How did you receive your call to write and speak?" And I looked at her and I said, "I haven't received a call to write or speak."

I felt everyone in there getting a little agitated—*If*

you haven't received a call, why are you here? I quickly prayed, "Lord, why am I here? When did you call me?" I had never even thought about it.

Just as quickly, he said, "Cynthia, don't you remember when you were twenty-two and I asked you to give me the steering wheel of your life? And you turned your life over to me? That was my call to you."

I shared a little bit with these women about my total surrender to Christ. We all must surrender daily, but I'm no longer driving the car of my life; God is. God's call on my life is to abide in him. It is to walk with him. It is to deepen my intimacy with him. Then *he* can direct my walk with him to use me as he pleases. And I think that's God's call on all of us.

These precious women come up to me and say, "God has called me to write and speak. What advice do you have?" And I say, "The best thing you can do is just stay close to Jesus. Walk with him, abide in him, and see." I always sign my emails "Keep Your Hand in His" because it's a great picture of staying connected to Christ, abiding in him. Oswald Chambers said, "Let God fling you out."[1] We don't have to try to manipulate things so that "Oh, I can speak" or "I can write." If God calls you, you want to be obedient. My challenge is for everyone to pray for God to lead them on the path that brings glory to his name. That's Psalm 23:3. That's what I pray.

I often ask a question that I've learned from reading Oswald Chambers: Am I willing to be even an obscure servant if that brings glory to God?[2] Writing and speaking seems so glamorous in the Christian world, and a lot of it is anointed and we need it. But I think sometimes our motives get mixed up, and we just need to be sure it's what God wants. We just want to be sure we're in the center of God's will.

JOYCE

You demonstrate in this book, *Becoming Like Jesus*, how the life of faith requires intentional submission to what God is teaching you. What is something God is teaching you these days?

CYNTHIA

I think right now he's just saying, "Cynthia, I am God and you are not, and I just need you to understand that life is not always lived on your terms. I love you and I am for you, and I want to continue to conform you to the image of my Son." One of my favorite quotations is from Erwin Lutzer, who says,

God . . . says, "I am that I am" (Ex. 3:14).
He is who He is and not who we want Him
to be.[3]

I think that's a great lesson to learn: that God has a
plan for us. That's what this book, *Becoming Like Jesus*,
is about. God's plan is to make us like Jesus, and his
ways are not our ways.

It's very freeing to let God be God in your life and
not try to take over or manipulate circumstances, but to
trust him. Years ago in a Hallmark store, I saw a magnet
that said, *Dear child, I can do it myself. Love, God.*

So over and over, over my life, over the years, I've
just said, "God, it's your life. It's not mine." More and
more I just realize that God is enough, God loves me, he
knows what he's doing, and I'm blessed to be his child.

JOYCE
I think that's the same thing he's teaching all of us—
whether you are a new Christian or you've been following him for your whole life. That surrendered *You
are God, and I am not.* Whatever situation we are in is
the same lesson. And we still have to go deeper in that.
You're eighty-four and you're still learning it, still going
to a deeper level in that surrender.

It sounds like for you, your writing has just flown, come out of your relationship with God, abiding in him, having your hand in his. And so it hasn't been that you've set out to write—it's that you've set out to walk with Jesus. Out of the overflow of that you're writing about the things he's teaching you in your relationship with him. That's really beautiful.

I think sometimes we can get the order wrong. We have these desires. And they may be godly desires to write Bible studies, but—and it can be slightly—our focus can go from abiding in Jesus to striving to do these things. It sounds like for you, the abiding part, staying in that place, has kept you in your heart's motivation to glorify him.

CYNTHIA

One time, I spoke at Wheaton College, and they had several photos of the studies and the words "Cynthia Heald wrote all this." I looked at that and thought, *I wonder how many people would come to hear Cynthia Heald, a homemaker who loves God?* I just think we need to be who God wants us to be. Who we are is more important to God than what we do. There's that verse: "Lord, we've prophesied, we've cast out demons, and we've done miracles in your name" (Matthew 7:22, author's paraphrase). And what did Jesus say? "I never knew you" (Matthew 7:23). It's not what we do; it's who we are. If we are who God wants us to be, then what we do *does* bring honor and glory to him.

Even if someone feels like God wants them to write, it could be yes, but it may take ten years. God is never in a hurry. It's his life, it's his way, and we just need to be faithful.

There's this great story—during a Billy Graham crusade in London, they sent pastors out to all the churches to speak. Well, this one pastor was given an assignment. He was given the address, then the taxi driver took him to the address and it was a factory. And the pastor said, "No, I'm supposed to be at a church." He said, "Sir, this is the address you gave me."

Finally, this one man came running up to the taxi and said, "Oh, pastor, I'm so glad you're here." The pastor got out of the taxi, and he couldn't see anything to speak to, any audience. The man gave him this little portable microphone. You see, during the fifteen-minute changes of the factory workers, the shifts, this man would preach. Sometimes the workers would stop and listen, but most of them just walked back and forth.

After the shift change, the visiting pastor asked, "How long have you been doing this?" The man said,

"Oh, fifteen years." And the pastor said, "How many have you seen come to Christ?" The man said, "Oh, a few. I have talked with many men, but that's about it." And the pastor said, "Oh, well, how can you stay here with this?" And the man said, "Oh, pastor, God didn't call me to be successful; he called me to be faithful."

It's not success or notoriety that we're after. We're after just pleasing God and being faithful to him and hearing "Well done."

JOYCE
As people are picking up *Becoming Like Jesus*, what would you like to say to people who are reading the book?

CYNTHIA
First Corinthians 10:31 says, "Whether you eat or drink, or whatever you do, do it all for the glory of God." And like in my experience in the jewelry store, I forget about representing Jesus. I forget about reflecting him in what Chambers called "the simple, shallow delights of life,"[4] like eating or grocery shopping. We meet someone at a checkout counter and move on. But I think we are supposed to be Jesus as much as we can, wherever we are. In a restaurant, does the person who waits on us know? Do they sense that we're kind and care about them?

I don't know how many times I've told God, "God, if I didn't love you, I wouldn't be doing this." If it's changing diapers or another mundane thing that I don't want to do, I want to respond in the best way I can that pleases him and brings him glory. I love when the Pharisees had questioned Peter and John and then afterward "they recognized that they had been with Jesus" (Acts 4:13, ESV). I hope that's our prayer—that anyone who crosses our path might recognize we have been with Jesus. I pray that we all go out there and are Christ's ambassadors wherever we are.

I know I've become so much more attentive. When I go to the grocery store, I engage the checkout person: "How are you today? How are things going?" One time this lady said, "Oh, my son's having surgery right now." I said, "Can I pray for you right now?" And I prayed for her while she was checking me out.

What I am encouraging myself with—and I feel like God is imprinting on my life—is that no matter what I do, I do it for him.

Becoming Like Jesus
Facilitator Guide

GOD DESIGNED US TO GROW not just individually in our relationship with him but also in community as we learn from and sharpen one another. If you choose to read and discuss this book as a six-week Bible study with your small group, this facilitator guide will offer you some encouragement and direction for your time together.

Facilitating a group doesn't require expertise or perfection—after all, we are all in the process of becoming like Jesus! Your group's purpose should be to provide insights, challenges, accountability, and prayer support for one another as you study God's Word and pursue Christlikeness in community. This pursuit is a lifelong process, but as you wholeheartedly seek to become like Jesus, you will be able to encourage one another with the growth and change that you see. I hope that when you finish the study, your group will not be the same as when you began!

To prepare yourself for the group experience, consider these activities:

1. Pray—for the Holy Spirit to guide the group members as they study, for each individual in your group, and for wisdom and grace for yourself as you lead the group.

2. As you study before each meeting, you might want to prepare specific questions for each section. You will find additional information and clarification in commentaries, a Bible dictionary, or other resources. Of course, your greatest resource is sensitivity to the Holy Spirit as he guides and directs the study according to the needs of the group.

If you opt to use the first meeting as a time for introductions, you might want to follow this suggested outline:

1. Have each member introduce themselves and share about their family and Christian experience.

2. Pass out the study books and look together at the format of the study. Note the table of contents and the structure of each lesson: the four key questions, quotations from Christian writers, personal applications, Scripture passages to read, and the author's concluding reflections.

3. Read the opening story in the author's "Opening Thoughts on Becoming Like Jesus," and reflect together on this question: *Am I faithful and kind in exemplifying Jesus' character with anyone I happen to encounter?*

4. Encourage group members to write the key verses for each lesson (under "How Did Jesus Live?") on index cards or Post-it notes, using their favorite Bible translations, and then place the verses where they will see them every day. You may wish to encourage group members to memorize one or more of the verses.

5. As a group, consider setting standards for your time together. These standards could include the commitment to attend the study, to read the Scripture verses, to answer the questions in each

lesson, and to be open about what God is revealing in your journeys toward Christlikeness.

6. Talk with the group about having prayer partners during the study. These partners would not have to meet together outside the group sessions, but they could share requests during the week.

7. At the end of your first meeting, ask the Holy Spirit to speak to each person's heart during the weeks of the study.

Later, as your group meets to discuss each lesson, you might use this structure:

1. Begin each session by asking the group members to share their key thoughts, new insights, or questions from the lessons.

2. Ask group members to share which of the Scripture passages was most meaningful to them and why.

3. Invite group members to share how they were able to apply the Scripture passages and new insights to their personal lives.

4. Pray together, asking group members to pray aloud, if they are comfortable. If your group has prayer partners, these people could spend a few minutes together sharing answers to prayer and praying for each other.

Notes

OPENING THOUGHTS ON BECOMING LIKE JESUS

1. W. Jones, "Christian Profession and Consequent Obligation" (homily on 1 John 2:6), in *The Pulpit Commentary*, vol. 22, eds. H. D. M. Spence and Joseph S. Exell (Peabody, MA: Hendrickson, n.d.), 54.
2. Oswald Chambers, *My Utmost for His Highest* (Westwood, NJ: Barbour, 1935), July 21.
3. Richard L. Strauss, *Growing More Like Jesus: A Practical Guide to Developing a Christlike Character* (Neptune, NJ: Loizeaux Brothers, 1991), 13.

LESSON ONE | GOD'S MASTER PLAN

1. J. R. Miller, *In Green Pastures: Devotional Readings for Every Day in the Year* (Fearn, Scotland: Christian Focus, 2005), December 26.
2. Warren W. Wiersbe, *The Wiersbe Bible Commentary: New Testament* (Colorado Springs: David C. Cook, 2007), 932.
3. Hannah Whitall Smith, *The Christian's Secret of a Happy Life* (Westwood, NJ: Revell, 1952), 103–4.

LESSON TWO | BEHOLDING

1. Donald Fraser, "The Christian Transfiguration" (homily on 2 Corinthians 3:18), in *The Pulpit Commentary*, vol. 19, eds. H. D. M. Spence and Joseph S. Exell (Peabody, MA: Hendrickson, 1985), 82.
2. J. R. Miller, *Making the Most of Life* (New York: Thomas Y. Crowell Co., 1891), 98.
3. Oswald Chambers, *My Utmost for His Highest* (Westwood, NJ: Barbour, 1935), May 14.

4. J. R. Miller, *In Green Pastures: Devotional Readings for Every Day in the Year* (Fearn, Scotland: Christian Focus, 2005), September 1.
5. Amy Carmichael, *Edges of His Ways: Daily Devotional Notes* (Fort Washington, PA: Christian Literature Crusade, 2011), April 29.

LESSON THREE | HOLY OBEDIENCE

1. Sam Storms, "The Commandments of God Are Not Burdensome! (Hebrews 12:12-17)" (sermon, Bridgeway Church, Oklahoma City, OK, March 1, 2015), https://www.samstorms.org/all-articles/post/the-commandments-of-god-are-not-burdensome-hebrews-1212-17.
2. Oswald Chambers, *My Utmost for His Highest* (Westwood, NJ: Barbour, 1935), May 13.
3. Warren W. Wiersbe, *The Wiersbe Bible Commentary: New Testament* (Colorado Springs: David C. Cook, 2007), 984.
4. Chambers, *My Utmost for His Highest*, July 9.
5. Andrew Murray, *The Path to Holiness* (Bloomington, MN: Bethany House, 2001), 55.
6. Robert Murray M'Cheyne, quoted in Warren Wiersbe, *50 People Every Christian Should Know: Learning from Spiritual Giants of the Faith* (Grand Rapids, MI: Baker Books, 2009), 85.
7. C. S. Lewis, *Letters to an American Lady*, ed. Clyde S. Kilby (Grand Rapids, MI: Eerdmans, 2014), 11.
8. The words translated "blessed" in both Hebrew (*'ashre*) and Greek (*makarios*) can also be translated "happy."

LESSON FOUR | A HUMBLE SERVANT

1. Andrew Murray, *Abide in Christ* (Colorado Springs: NavPress, 2019), 133.

LESSON FIVE | UNCONDITIONAL LOVE

1. Kenneth Wuest, quoted in Bruce Hurt, "Love-Agape (Greek Word Study)," Precept Austin, updated July 26, 2023, https://www.preceptaustin.org/love-agape.
2. Bruce Hurt, "Love-Agape (Greek Word Study)," https://www.preceptaustin.org/love-agape.

3. Maurice E. Wagner, quoted in William M. Fletcher, *The Second Greatest Commandment* (Colorado Springs: NavPress, 1983), 31.

LESSON SIX | TRUSTING GOD'S PLAN

1. Oswald Chambers, *My Utmost for His Highest* (Westwood, NJ: Barbour, 1935), July 22.
2. Warren W. Wiersbe, *The Wiersbe Bible Commentary: New Testament* (Colorado Springs: David C. Cook, 2007), 268.
3. J. R. Miller, *In Green Pastures: Daily Readings for Every Day in the Year* (Fearn, Scotland: Christian Focus, 2005), February 20.
4. Miller, *In Green Pastures*, November 25.

CLOSING THOUGHTS ON BECOMING LIKE JESUS

1. W. Ian Thomas, *The Indwelling Life of Christ: All of Him in All of Me* (Colorado Springs: Multnomah Books, 2006), 130.

A CONVERSATION WITH CYNTHIA HEALD

1. Oswald Chambers, *My Utmost for His Highest* (Westwood, NJ: Barbour, 1935), March 11.
2. "We want to be able to say, 'Oh, I have had a wonderful call from God!' But to do even the most humbling tasks to the glory of God takes the Almighty God Incarnate working in us. To be utterly unnoticeable requires God's Spirit in us making us absolutely humanly His. The true test of a saint's life is not successfulness but faithfulness on the human level of life. We tend to set up success in Christian work as our purpose, but our purpose should be to display the glory of God in human life, to live a life 'hidden with Christ in God' in our everyday human conditions (Colossians 3:3). Our human relationships are the very conditions in which the ideal life of God should be exhibited." Oswald Chambers, *My Utmost for His Highest*, ed. James Reimann, updated ed. (Grand Rapids, MI: Discovery House Publishers, 1992), November 16.

3. Erwin Lutzer, "When God Comes" (sermon), Heart-Cry for Revival Conference, April 2002, Asheville, NC, https://www.sermonindex.net/modules/articles/index.php?view=article&aid=28292.

4. Chambers, *My Utmost for His Highest*, updated ed., November 22.

Become the Woman God Created You to Be

BOOKS BY
CYNTHIA HEALD

Bible teacher and bestselling author Cynthia Heald draws on several decades of faith to share foundational truths to help you walk hand in hand with Jesus.

"Cynthia is a gentle guide, showing us how to walk the 'narrow way' with her wisdom, experience, and grace. She has learned from the Master how to walk in true freedom, and I'm grateful for her heart to lead us to his feet."
- Jessie Minassian, author of *Unashamed*